Effective Revision
The guide to courses and resources

FIRST EDITION

Edited by Sue Fryer

Careerscope Guides

ISBN 0 901936 98 7
February 2005

www.careerscope.info

Design: Philip Gray
Text set in Arial 10 on 12pt
Print: Print Solutions Partnership

© *CAREERSCOPE GUIDES 2005*
February 2005

12A Princess Way, Camberley, Surrey GUI5 35P
Tel: 01276 21188   Fax: 01276 691833
Email: sylvie.pool@isco.org.uk
www.careerscope.info

Effective Revision

CONTENTS

" Revise: to study again something you have already learned, in preparation for an exam....to look at or consider again, an idea, piece of writing etc. in order to correct or improve it...."

Welcome to the first edition of Effective Revision: the guide to courses and resources. Although the book contains details of traditional 'revision course' providers, such as the long established tutorial colleges, it recognises that we are in the 'e-learning' age and that some readers will be happy to learn or revise via a book or website.

Why is there a need for a book about Revision?

We live in a competitive age where many students/learners are under tremendous pressure to gain top or specified exam grades in order to get onto to the course of their choice; failing to do so could mean that they cannot train for their desired career. For some, a few percentage points can make the crucial difference between meeting or failing to meet course or employer entry requirements. Some employers of graduates still look back to an applicant's GCSE grades, as well as A level or degree performance, so the pressure to achieve starts an early age. Not all students will enter Higher education, but the majority will still need exam passes in order to train for a career or progress to Further education.

Consolidating knowledge, revising and reinforcing essential concepts and facts and learning how to prepare for exams are processes that all students need assistance with.

This book is for all learners, whatever their level or background and therefore includes a vast range of revision help and resources ranging from the expensive to the totally free.

Traditional revision courses

Why would students benefit from attending a revision course?

Any learner may fit into one or more of the following categories:

- *Under-confident about elements of the syllabus they have studied*
- *Needing to consolidate, clarify or 'revisit' topics and issues previously studied*
- *Feeling they have some gaps in knowledge that need remedying*

- Needing to gain top grades for entry to the course of their choice
- Wanting to gain understanding of their strong and weak areas of knowledge
- Wanting to make up for not working steadily enough throughout their course
- Wanting specialised/expert tips for the subject(s) being studied
- Wanting tips and hints on exam technique
- Wishing to take some 'mock exams' to get them into 'exam mode'
- Wanting to revise in the company of fellow-students, with an experienced tutor on hand
- Preferring to revise in a new environment away from their usual teachers/classmates

Nowadays, the traditional attendance-based 'Easter revision' courses may also be offered at Christmas, Summer, or indeed, throughout the year. Many colleges offer residential facilities if required. Most of the relevant websites give full details of fees, accreditation, accommodation, tutorial staff and subjects and examination boards offered; all will send course brochures on request. For details of these courses go to Section two for an updated list of course providers, subdivided into provider category.

Internet resources

This section provides an overview of the myriad of Internet-based revision resources and websites, many of which are interactive. Some are 'revision overview' sites, giving links to a wide range of resources; some are subject specific whilst others are interactive or tutorial in intent. Some sites fulfil all three functions. Many are totally free to use whilst some ask for a fee to use the interactive parts of the site. Overall, they provide an astonishing amount of revision material and shouldn't be overlooked.

A reminder: the Internet is an unregulated medium and therefore students or parents are urged to 'check out' the site credentials before parting with details such personal information and credit card payments. Please read the NOTES FOR PARENTS relating to safe use of the Internet at the beginning of Section three.

Books, CD-ROMS and other resources

For those preferring conventional printed/audio-visual resources etc, Section 4 gives a selection of the huge range of available titles. Go to Section 4 Revision resources

What are revision theories and techniques?

Go to Section 5 for an overview of major revision theories and techniques. Everyone can discover their Personal Learning style (for free) and plot their revision style and methodology accordingly!

Accreditation/ quality assurance

Check out Section 6 to check on accreditation or quality assurance issues relating to revision course providers/resources.

Examination boards

Section 7 is a list of the relevant exam boards - essential addresses for obtaining past papers and other information.

And finally, to all learners – Good Luck with those exams!

Choosing a course - Checklist

Before you decide where to go for your revision course, do some research to make sure it is the right choice for you. Make sure you can tick all of the following boxes on the check-list. Remember that in most cases, revision courses themselves are not accredited or monitored by any official body; look instead for accreditation of the institution that is running them (see also Section six: Accreditation of Providers).

✓ with the answer to this question

☐ Is the school or college accredited; if it is, is there an inspection report published within the last five years available to read? (see also Section 6 of this book)

☐ How long have they been teaching revision courses? Are the teachers experienced revision tutors? (The website/ prospectus should give this information)

☐ Is there a revision courses director/department? Is there anyone you can speak to about your requirements, problems or issues before enrolling?

☐ Are the courses targeted at your particular syllabus or exam board?

☐ What were last year's pass rates for the level of course and subject(s) that you want to revise? Can you find this information on the website or in the prospectus?

☐ Have they ever cancelled a course due to low take-up of numbers? How much notice would they give of cancellation?

☐ What are class sizes? (the smaller the better) How many hours of teaching are there per day?

☐ If you need residential accommodation, can you view it in the prospectus or on their website - perhaps by a virtual tour - or coould you visit beforehand?

☐ If you are staying residentially, are there teachers or staff on site 24/7? (This may not be relevant if you are staying with a host family rather than in centre/college accommodation)

Providers of revision courses for GCSE, AS, A2, IB and Scottish examinations

Providers are listed alphabetically in the following categories

a. Schools

b. Tutorial colleges and Independent 6th form colleges

c. Universities: revision, taster and Summer courses

d. Specialist subject courses (courses run in UK)

e. Specialist subject courses (run outside the UK)

f. Private tutors – how to locate

Online tuition/interactive revision websites are listed in Section 3

Schools

Clifton College

32 College Road, Clifton Bristol , BS 8 3JH
Tel: 0117 973 9187
Web: www.cliftoncollegeuk.com
Easter revision courses for GCSEs/A2/A levels

Harrow Easter Revision Courses

Harrow School, Harrow on the Hill, Harrow HA1 3HP
Tel: 020 8426 4638
Web: www.harrowschool.org.uk/ revision/Easterrevision
GCSE, AS and A2 Easter courses

King's International Study Centre

The King's School, Ely, Cambridgeshire CB7 4 DB
Tel: 01353 653600
Web: www.kisc-ely.com
GCSE Easter revision

Magdalen Court School

Mulberry House, Victoria Park Road, Exeter, Devon EX2 4NU
Tel: 01392 494919
GCSE/AS/A revision courses

Millfield Enterprises

Butleigh Road, Street, Somerset BA16 0YD
Tel: 01458 444458
Web: www.millfieldenterprises.com
GCSE/AS,A2 Easter revision courses

Oakham School

Chapel Close, Oakham, Rutland LE15 6DT
Tel: 01572 758758
Web: www.oakham.org.uk or www.ibicus.org.uk
Revision courses for IB, GCSE, AS, A2

Rochester Independent College

Star Hill, Kent ME1 1XF
Tel: 01634 828115
Web: www.rochester-college.org
Easter revision/resits. GCSE, AS, A2

Taunton School

Taunton, Somerset TA2 6AD
Tel: 01823 349223
Web: www.tauntonschool.co.uk
GCSE, AS, A2, Easter revision courses

Wellington College

Crowthorne, Berkshire RG45 7PU
Tel: 01344 771 147
Web: www.wellington-college.berks.sch.uk
Easter revision courses for GCSE/AS/A2

The following organizations offer individual search facilities to assist enquirers to identify UK schools offering revision courses :

Isbi *(Web: www.isbi.com) Click on Revision/retake courses.* This takes you to a online 'personal enquiry form' searchable by location and exam level/subject.

Gabbitas *(Web: www.gabbitas.co.uk) Click on Education 11-18* then to exam preparation and revision. A personal search form is available for completion.

Tutorial colleges and independent sixth form colleges

Abacus College and the Oxford Language Centre

Threeways House, George Street, Oxford OX1 2BJ
Tel: 01865 240111
Web: www.abacuscollege.net
Email: principal@abacuscollege.net
AS /A2 resits of 1 term- one year duration

Abbey College Birmingham

10 St Paul's Square, Birmingham, West Midlands B3 1QU
Tel: 0121 2367474
Web: www.abbeycolleges.co.uk
Email: via website
GCSE, AS and A2, Easter Revision courses offered during school holidays at all Abbey colleges

Abbey College Cambridge

17 Station Rd, Cambridge CB1 2JB
Tel: 01223 578280
Web: www.abbeycolleges.co.uk
Email: via website
GCSE, AS and A2, Easter Revision courses offered during school holidays at all Abbey colleges

Abbey College London

28A Hereford Road, London W2 5AJ
Tel: 0207 229528
Web: www.abbeycolleges.co.uk
Email: via website
GCSE, AS and A2, Easter Revision courses offered during school holidays at all Abbey colleges

Abbey College Manchester

Cheapside, King Street, Manchester M2 4WG
Tel: 0161 817 2700
Web: www.abbeycolleges.co.uk
Email: via website
GCSE, AS and A2, Easter Revision courses offered during school holidays at all Abbey colleges

Albany College

24 Queen's Road Hendon London NW4 2TL
0208 202 5965
Web: www.albany-college.co.uk
Email: mary@albany-college.co.uk
Individually tailored 3 month revision courses for students wishing to re-sit AS and A2 units in January.

Academy Revision

41 Finsbury Stree, Alford, Lincolnshire LN13 9BH
Tel: 01507 466 141
Web: www.eastercourses/info
Academy Revision provides revision courses at Leeds and Nottingham for GCSE, AS, A2. Courses are FREE for parents on income support and students who have suffered from serious illness in exam year.

Ashbourne Independent 6th form college

17 Old Court Place, London, W8 4 PL
Tel: 020 7 7937 3858
Web: www.ashbournecollege.co.uk
Email: admin@ashbournecollege.co.uk
GCSE, AS and A2 Easter revision courses

Bales College

742 Harrow Road, London W10 4AA
Tel: 020 8960 5899
Web: www.balescollege.co.uk
Email: info@balescollege.co.uk
Offers one year intensive A level retake courses

Basil Paterson Tutorial College

22-23 Abercromby Place, Edinburgh, EH3 6QE
Tel: 0131 556 7698
Web: www.basilpaterson.co.uk
Email: info@basilpaterson.co.uk
Easter revision/Intensive one-term re-sits/private tuition/for GCSEs, Scottish Highers and A Levels.

Providers

Bellerbys College Cambridge

Arbury Rd, Cambridge CB4 2JF
Tel: 01223 517037
Web: www.bellerbys.com
Email: hove@bellerbys.com
Full range of courses for international students wishing to progress to higher education in UK

Bellerbys College London

Downshire House, Roehampton Lane, London SW15 4HT
Tel: 020 8780 0841
Web: www.bellerbys.com
Email: hove@bellerbys.com
Full range of courses for international students wishing to progress to higher education in UK

Bellerbys College Brighton and Hove

44 Cromwell Road, Hove, East Sussex BN3 3ER
Tel: 01273 723911
Web: www.bellerbys.com
Email: hove@bellerbys.com
Full range of courses for international students wishing to progress to higher education in UK

Bellerbys College Oxford

9 Blue Boar Street, Oxford OX1 4EZ
Tel: 01865 205077
Web: www.bellerbys.com
Email: hove@bellerbys.com
Full range of courses for international students wishing to progress to higher education in UK

Bosworth Independent College

Nazareth House, Barrack Road, Northampton NN2 6AF
Tel: 01604 239 995
www.bosworthcollege.com
Email: mkt2@bosworthcollege.com
GCSE, AS/ A2 Easter revision courses (2 days for each subject)

Brampton College (formerly The Tuition Centre)

Lodge House, Hendon, London NW4 OAH
Tel: 0208 203 5025
Web: www.bramptoncollege.com
Email: enqs@bramptoncollege.com
GCSE one year re-sits, 1 term/one year A level Re-sits.

Brooke House College

Leicester Road, Market Harborough, Leicester LE16 7AU
Tel: 01858 462452
Web: www.brookehouse.com
Email: brookehse@aol.com
Easter revision for GCSE AS and A2

Cambridge Arts and Sciences

13-14 Round Church Street, Cambridge CB5 8AD
Tel: 01223 314431
Web: www.easter-revision.com (revision courses site)
Web: www.catscollege.co.uk (college main site)
Email: enquiries@easter-revision.com
Website packed with useful revision advice. Lists exam boards,
syllabus information for GCSE, AS/ A2 subjects.

Cambridge Centre for 6th Form Studies

1 Salisbury Villas, Station Road, Cambridge CB1 2JF
Tel: 01223 716890
Web: www.ccss.co.uk click on Easter revision
Email: enquiries@ccss.co.uk
Online syllabus and module information for GCSE, AS and A2
revision courses held at Easter. 2 subjects covered per week.

Cambridge Seminars

4 Hawthorne Way, Cambridge CB4 1AX
Tel: 01223 313464
Web: www.camsem.co.uk
Email: admissions@camsem.co.uk
One year A level resits.

Cambridge Tutors College

Water Tower Hill, Croydon, Surrey CR0 5SX
Tel: 0208 688 5284
Web: www.ctc.ac.uk click on Foundation and revision courses
Email: admin@ctc.ac.uk
12-16 week study skills courses including Revision Technique.
Syllabus/exam board info.

Campbell Harris Tutors

185 Kensington High Street, London W8 6SH
Tel: 0207 9370032
Web: www.campbellharris.com
Email: principal@campbellharris.com
Easter and Christmas Revision courses GCSE/AS/A2

Cardiff Academy

40-41 The Parade, Cardiff CF 24 3AB
Tel: 029 2040 9630
Web: www.cardiffacademy.org.uk
Email: 40-41@theparade.fsbusiness.co.uk
One year GCSE and one year A level re-sits

Clifton Tutors Ltd

31 Pembroke Road, Clifton, Bristol BS8 3BE
Tel: 0117 973 8376
Web: www.cliftontutors.co.uk
Email: wpshaw@btinternet.com
GCSE, AS/ A2 Exam prep. One-to-one tuition.

Cherwell College

The Masters Lodgings, Greyfriars Paradise St. Oxford OX1 1LD
Tel: 01865 242670
Web: www.cherwell-college.co.uk (Easter Intensive courses)
Email: secretary@cherwell-college.co.uk
GCSE, AS/ A2 subjects; Online request for Revision course information.

Collingham 5th and 6th Form School and College

23 Collingham Gardens, London SW5 0HL
Tel: 0207 244 7414
Web: www.collingham.co.uk click on Easter revision courses
Email: london@collingham.co.uk
Easter and Christmas revision courses for GCSE, AS, A2 courses. Private tuition, one day workshops, and Summer study skills course also available

David Game College

69 Notting Hill Gate, London W11 3JS
Tel: 020 7 221 6665
Web: www.davidgame-group.com
Email: info@davidgame-group.com
GCSE intensive re-sits/private tuition offered all year.

Davies, Laing and Dick

100 Marylebone Lane, London W1U 2QB
Tel: 020 7375 8411
Web: www.dld.org click on Easter revision
Email: dld@dld.org
Details of Easter revision courses and enrolment form on website. Private tuition available all year.

Dean College

97-101 Seven Sisters Road, London N7 7QP
Tel: 0207 281 4461/2
Web: www.deancollege.co.uk
Email: deancollege@aul.edu
GCSE/A level Easter Revision and intensive six month re-sit courses

Duff-Miller

59 Queen's Gate, London SW7 5JP
020 7225 0577
Web: www.duffmiller.com
Email: enqs@duffmiller.com
Easter revision for GCSE/AS/A2. See also section 5b

Ealing Independent College

83 New Broadway, London W5 5AL
Tel: 0208 579 6668
Web: www.ealingindependentcollege.com
Email: ealingcollege@btconnect.com
Intensive AS/A2 resits. Also 1:1 private tuition in all subjects.

Edward Greene's Tutorial Establishment

45 Pembroke Street, Oxford OX1 1BP
Tel: 01865 248 308
Web: www.edward-greene.ac.uk click on Revision courses
Email: registrar@edward-greene.ac.uk
GSCE/ A2/ AS Easter revision courses. All tuition is individual.

Exeter Tutorial College

44-46 Magdalen Road, Exeter, Devon EX2 4TE
Tel: 01392 278101
Web: www.tutorialcollege.com click on Exams
Email: info@tutorialcollege.com
Study skills, A level resits

Fast Forward Revision School

33 Langdon Road, Rochester, Kent ME1 1UN
Courses based at Cobham Hall, North Kent
Tel: 01634 400892
Web: www.ffrevision.co.uk
Email: ffrs@supanet.com
GCSE, AS, A2 Easter revision courses.

Harrogate Tutorial College

2 The Oval, Harrogate, North Yorkshire HG2 9BA
Tel: 01423 501 041
Web: www.htcuk.org click on Easter revision
Email study@htcuk.org
Easter revision in over 30 subjects at CGSE and A level.
Also One year intensive A level re-sits, Study skills, Pre- Medical school, Maths for scientists and ICT for A level students.

Irwin College

164 London Road, Leicester LE2 IND
Tel: 0116 255 2648
Web: www.cife.org.uk/irwin/index.htm
Email: enquiries@irwincollege.tele2.co.uk
Specialist Foundation course in Medical studies

Justin Craig Education (Specialist Revision College)

13 High St, Colney Heath, St Albans, Herts AL4 ONS
Tel: 01727 827 000
Web: www.justincraig.ac.uk
Email: via website
Revision for Yr 10,GSCE AS/A2 Easter and Spring courses.
Plus online revision tips.

Lansdowne Independent College

40-44 Bark Place, London W2 4AT
Tel: 020 7616 4400
Web: www.lansdownecollege.com click on Easter revision
Email: education@lansdownecollege.com
Short retake A level courses;one year intensive A level resits;
Medical School preparation course

Macclesfield Tutorial College

20 Cumberland Street, Macclesfield, Cheshire SK10 1DD
Tel: 01625 501440
Web: www.macctc.co.uk
Half term and Easter revision courses at GCSE, AS, A2 and
undergraduate levels. Includes unusual subjects such as
Russian, Chinese.

Mander Portman Woodward Birmingham

38 Highfield Road, Edgbaston, Birmingham B15 3ED
Tel: 0121 454 9637
Web: www.mpw.co.uk click on Easter revision courses
Email: enq@birmingham.mpw.co.uk
Easter revision; Extra coaching over Summer and during half-
terms; Jan-June retakes; Medical school entry preparation; A
level one year resits.

Mander Portman Woodward Cambridge

3/4 Brookside, Cambridge CB2 1JE
Tel: 01223 350 158
Web: www.mpw.co.uk click on Easter revision courses
Email: enquiries@cambridge.mpw.co.uk
Easter revision; Extra coaching over Summer and during half-
terms; Jan-June retakes; Medical school entry preparation; A
level one year resits.

Mander Portman Woodward London

90-92 Queen's Gate, London SW7 5AB
Tel: 0207 835 1355
Web: www.mpw.co.uk click on Easter revision courses
Email: london@mpw.co.uk

Easter revision; Extra coaching over Summer and during half-terms; Jan-June retakes; Medical school entry preparation; A level one year resits.

Modes Study Centre

73-75 George Street, Oxford OX1 2BQ
Tel: 01865 245172
Web: www.cife.org.uk/modes   Email: modes@cife.org.uk
Specialists in Maths and science subjects. Intensive resits and one year A level courses

D'Overbroeck's College

1 Park Town, Oxford OX2 6SN
Tel: 01865 310000
Web: www.doverbroecks.com click on Easter Revision
Email: via website
GCSE, AS, A2 Easter revision

Oxford Easter Courses

98 Southmoor Road, Oxford OX2 6RB
Tel: 01865 311517
Web: http://ds.dial.pipex.com/oec/   Email: oec@dial.pipex.com
AS, A2 and IB Easter revision courses at St Hilda's College.

Oxford Individual Tuition

39 Kennett Road, Headington, Oxford OX3 7BH
Tel: 01865 763065
Web: www.headington.org.uk/businesses/tutors - Click on Vacation revision and Easter revision
Email: jenkins@cornmarket.co.uk
Half-term, w/end and after-school tuition available. Christmas and Easter revision courses.

Oxford International College

Southern House, 1 Cambridge Terrace, Oxford OX1 1RR
Tel: 01865 203988
Web: www.oxcoll.com - see vacation courses link
Email: info@oxcoll.com
Easter and Christmas revision courses for GCSE, A level and IB.

Oxford Science Studies

Southern House, 1 Cambridge Terrace, Oxford 0X1 3HJ
Tel: 01453 752361
Web: www.oxss.co.uk
Email: info@oxss.co.uk
GCSE, A level and IB - offer 3 residential revision courses a year- Easter, Summer, Christmas. Most subjects covered.

Oxford School of Learning

66 Sunderland Avenue, Oxford OX2 8DU
Tel: 01865 412 428
Web: www.osl-ltd.co.uk - click on About OSL
Email: info@osl-ltd.co.uk
Business and economics are main subjects. Group and individual tuition. Free revision notes and online tuition sections.

Oxford Tutorial College

12 King Edward Street, Oxford OX1 4HT
Tel: 01865 793 333
Web: www.otc.ac.uk click on Easter revision
Email: info@otc.ac.uk
AS and A2 Easter revision courses held at Brasenose college. Also: study skills and exam technique; A level re-sits.

Oxfordshire College of International Education

4 Hythe Bridge Street, Oxford OX1 2EP
Tel: 01865 202238
Web: www.cie-oxford.com
Email: info@cie-oxford.com
Revision courses. For groups/Individuals/All year

Philip Allan Updates

Market Place, Deddington Oxfordshire OX15 0SE
Tel: 01869 338 652
Web: www.philipallan.co.uk Click on Student events
Email: sales@philipallan.co.uk
Intensive revision for AS/A2 courses also one day Student conferences - insights into particular subjects. Publisher of various subject-specific educational resources.

The Physics Tuition Company

94 Sandygate Road, Sheffield S10 5RZ
Tel: 0794 1601673
Web: www.physicstuition.co.uk
Email: rolleys@tiscali.co.uk
Easter and Spring bank holiday revision courses for GCSE Chem, Maths and Physics GCSE, AS and A2. Also Saturday Physics GCSE, AS, A2 Tuition courses.

Regent College

Sai House, 167 Imperial Drive, Harrow, Middlesex HA2 7JP
Tel: 0208 933 5410
Web: www.rtc.uk.net click on Easter revision
Email: info@rtc.uk.net
A level re-sits in six months/one year Private tuition always available. Easter revision for SAT, GCSE, AS and A level

Rochester Independent College

3 New Road, Rochester, Kent ME1 1BD
Tel: 01634 828 115
Web: www.rochester-college.org Click on Courses - Easter revision
Email: admissions@rochester-college.org
Easter revision for GCSE, AS and A2 .Also re-sits, after-school classes and revision help in study-leave periods.

St Clare's Oxford International Baccalaureate Centre

139 Banbury Road, Oxford OX2 7 AL
Tel: 01865 5552 031
Web: www.stclares.ac.uk
Email: admissions@stclares.ac.uk
Easter and Summer revision for IB courses only

Scott Hurd

Contact via website
Web: www.scott-hurd.co.uk
Email: scott.hurd@virgin.net
Groupwork tuition in examination and revision skills

Surrey College

Abbot House, Sydenham Road, Guildford, Surrey GU1 3RL
Tel: 01483 565887
Web: www.ge-group.co.uk
Email: mail@surrey-college.co.uk
Easter and Christmas revision courses. For GCSE, AS/ A2. Private tuition available all year.

Surrey Tutors

Connaught House, 56 Connaught Road, Fleet, Hants GU S1 3LP
Tel: 01932 855051
Web: www.surreytutors.co.uk Go to Easter revision courses
GSCE, AS, A2 courses: Farnham, Surrey; Guildford, Surrey;
Bayswater, London; Alton, Hampshire; New Malden, Greater
London; Carshalton, Greater London

Tutorial College of West London

39-47 High St, Southall, Middlesex UB1 3 HF
Tel: 0208 571 9900
Web: www.tcwl.co.uk
Email: enquiries@tcwl.co.uk
GCSE, AS, A2 resits.

Wallace College

12 George IV Bridge, Edinburgh, Midlothian EH1 1EE
Tel: 0131 220 3634
Web: www.wallacecollege.co.uk Click on Easter revision courses
Email: info@wallacecollege.co.uk
Easter revision for Scottish Standards, Highers, AS and A2.
Individual tuition for A level students.

Wessex Tutors

44 Shirley Road, Southampton S015 3EU
Tel: 023 8033 4719
Web: www.wessextutors.com - see courses offered
Email: enquiries@wessextutors.com
Easter revision courses for A/S, A2 levels and GCSE

Westminster Tutors

86 Old Brompton Road, London SW7 3LQ
Tel: 0207 584 1288
Web: www.westminstertutors.co.uk
Email: info@westminstertutors.co.uk
Easter and Christmas revision courses for AS/A2. Individual tuition available all year.

Universities offering revision, taster and summer courses

Univertsity revision courses

The listing in this section was obtained through detailed university website searches.

Few of these sites have prominent references to revision courses, therefore some relevant courses may have been inadvertently omitted from this guide.

Many departmental level pages, particularly language departments, do include revision courses: you may discover more as you travel around the Net!

University of Wales, Aberystwyth

Old College, King Street, Aberystwyth, Ceredigion SY23 2AX
Tel: 01970 622065
Web: www.aberystwyth.ac.uk/en/schools
Email: hdm@aber.ac.uk
Follow links to Schools and colleges Liason service then click on link to Academic departments programme. An entry here describes 'lectures, presentations and workshops' on a wide variety of academic subjects.

Birmingham University Centre for Modern Lnguages

Edgbaston, Birmingham B15 2TT
Tel: 0121 414 3324
Web: www.cml.bham.ac.uk
Email: schools-liaison@bham.ac.uk
Click on GCSE/A level revision courses (Modern Languages).
Easter revision courses in GCSE and AS and A2 courses

Liverpool John Moores University

Roscoe Court, 4 Rodney Street, Liverpool L1 2TZ
Tel: 0151 231 3668 (specific to revision courses)
Web: www.livjm.ac.uk
Email: recruitment@livjm.ac.uk (general)
Intensive Easter revision courses in key subjects at AS/A levels

University of Manchester

Oxford Road, Manchester M13 9PL
Tel: 0161 275 2077
Web: www.manchester.ac.uk
Email: recruit.events@man.ac.uk
Go to Calendar of events, then click on subject-related events .
Courses such as 'UBEST languages GCSE-AS-A2 gap-bridging
events for years 11-12, held in the Summer.'

University of Nottingham

University Park, Nottingham NG7 2RD
Tel 0115 8466 358
Web: www.nottingham.ac.uk/modernlanguages
Email: undergraduate-enquiries@nottingham.ac.uk
Click on Academic Learning services, then on Easter revision.
GCSE, AS and A2 small-group courses for French, German,
Italian, Spanish

Oxford Brookes University

Gipsy Lane, Headington, Oxford OX3 0BP
Tel: 01865 484848
Web: www.brookes.ac.uk/schoolsandcolleges
Email: query@brookes.ac.uk
For Masterclass programmes in various academic subjects for Years 11,12 and 13 visit www.ah.brookes.ac.uk/languages/services - click on Revision weekend courses. Regular, intensive AS and A2 revision for Italian, French, German and Spanish.

University of Sheffield

Palmerston Rd, Sheffield S10 2TE
Tel:0114 2226296
Web: www.shef.ac.uk/english/natcect
Email: study@sheffield.ac.uk
The National centre for English cultural tradition (Natcect) offers study days/seminars for those studying English Language A level.

Swansea Institute of Higher Education

Mount Pleasant, Swansea SA1 6ED
Tel: 01792 481000
Web: www.sihe.ac.uk
Email: enquiry@sihe.ac.uk
Biennial 1-day 6th form Revision conference in Business studies, aimed at Year12/13 pupils studying A level or equivalent. Takes place twice a year, in November and in June. For details contact Charles Smith on 01792 481159 or email charles.smith@sihe.ac.uk

University of Warwick (Language Centre)

Coventry CV4 7AL
Tel: 024 7652 3462
Web: www.warwick.ac.uk/fac/arts/languagecentre/courses
Three day Easter revision course for AS and A2

University of the West of England, Bristol

Coldharbour Lane, Bristol BS16 1QY
Web: www.uwe.ac.uk - click on News, then events
Email: admissions@uwe.ac.uk
Courses such as Maths event day, GCSE into Science and
History A level day.

University taster and summer courses

For an overview of this type of course,
please read the detailed section on
taster courses in **The Sixthformer's
Guide**, published by Careerscope.

For details please visit the bookshop at www.careerscope.info

University of Cambridge - Continuing Education

Madingley Hall, Madingley, Cambridge, CB3 8AQ
Web: www.cont-ed.cam.ac.uk
Email: intenq@cont-ed.cam.ac.uk
The Institute of Continuing Education offers a wide range of
subject courses, short courses and day schools which may
match individual revision requirements.

NAGTY (National Association for Gifted and Talented Youth)

Providers

NAGTY, The University of Warwick, Coventry CV4 7AL

Tel: 024 7657 4760

Web: www.warwick.ac.uk/gifted

Email: nagty-cpd@warwick.ac.uk

NAGTY offers a programme of summer schools which are run at the following universities:

* Canterbury
* Exeter
* Durham
* Imperial
* Lancaster
* Warwick

NAGTY members can also access other specialist services i.e. Maths online study group, where students can get help with Maths homework/problems, run through Warwick university.

Exscitec

PO Box 92, Petersfield GU31 4YF

Tel: 01730 262927

Web: www.exscitec.com

Email: online@exscitec.com

Exscitec organise summer schools for years 6-11 in science technology; Year 12 and 13 MasterClasses ie.10 day Medical and Biological sciences. Masterclass held at Imperial college in July.

Greenwich University

Old Royal Naval College, Park Row, Greenwich SE10 9LS

Tel: 020 8331 8000

www.gre.ac.uk/summer/courses

Effective learning skills; Maths bridge; Introduction to science.

Headstart Courses

Weltech Centre, Ridgeway, Welwyn Garden City, Herts AL7 2AA
Tel: 01707 871505
Web: www.headstart.org.uk
Email: enquiries@headstartcourses.org.uk
Four day residential science and technology courses held at university locations throughout the UK: Bath, Birmingham, Bristol, Cambridge, Cardiff, Durham, Glamorgan, Heriot-Watt, Hull, Imperial, Lancaster, Leeds, Liverpool, Loughborough, Manchester, Newcastle, Nottingham, Nottingham, Oxford, Southampton

University of London Taster Courses

University of London
Tel: 0207 782 8034 for details of all courses
Email:tastercourses@lon.ac.uk
Wide range of free short courses in variety of subjects such as: Women in Mathematics, Introduction to Medicine. For details/ to obtain copy of Taster course booklet, contact: Mrs P. Evans, University of London, Tel 0207 782 8034

Specialist subject revision courses run in the UK - listed by subject

A selection of an ever-growing number of courses

Chemistry

Freerevision

8 Rowstock, Oseney Crescent, London NW5 2BA
Tel: 0207 485 3233
Web: www.freerevision.com
Chemistry only: Easter revision/Edexcel board/AS and A level

Languages

Numerous language courses are available, both UK-based and International. Some providers offer specific revision courses; others offer short intensive courses which may be of value for revision purposes. Many providers also arrange individual tuition.

The following section includes UK-based organisations. Other language course providers are included in the later section on revision courses outside the UK section - see page 35.

See also the companion Carrerscope Guide **Study Gap** which lists over 100 European language course providers

Study Gap

For details please visit the bookshop at www.careerscope.info

Alliance Française London

14 Cromwell Place, London SW7 2JR
Tel: 020 7581 2701
Web: www.institut-francais.org.uk
Email: language-centre@ambafrance.org.uk
GCSE, AS & A level revision courses

Alliance Française Glasgow

2-3 Park Circus, Glasgow G3 6AX
Tel: 0141 331 4080
Web: www.afglasgow.org.uk
Email: classes@afglasgow.org.uk
French exam review workshops, oral revision courses, Easter and Summer revision for Standard, Higher and Advanced levels.

Bridge House Languages

4 Old Bridge House Road, Bursledon, Southampton SO31 8AJ
Tel: 02380 405827
Web: www.bridgehouse.btinternet.co.uk
Email: bridgehouse@btinternet.com
GCSE revision and A level preparation courses in various European languages.

Mathematics

MathsMasters

Tel: 0870 765 1030
Web: www.mathsmasters.com
Email: enquiries@mathsmasters.com
Maths revision seminars weekend courses, online tutoring for GCSE/A level.

Medical and veterinary school preparation

Collingham

23 Collingham Gardens, London SW5 0HL
Tel: 0207 244 7414
Web: www.collingham.co.uk click on Medical entry programme
Email: london@collingham.co.uk

Duff-Miller

59 Queen's Gate, London SW7 5JP
020 7225 0577
Web: www.duffmiller.com
Email: enqs@duffmiller.com

Ealing Independent College

83 New Broadway, London W5 5AL
Tel: 0208 579 6668
Web: www.ealingindependentcollege.com
Email: ealingcollege@btconnect.com
Medical sciences preparation course

Exscitec

PO Box 92, Petersfield GU31 4YF
Tel: 01730 262927
Web: www.exscitec.com
Email: online@exscitec.com
Summer courses: Medical and Biological sciences MasterClass
10 day course in Summer, for students interested in Medicine as a
Career. Other MasterClasses for Years 12 and 13 at other locations.

Harrogate Tutorial College

2 The Oval, Harrogate, North Yorkshire HG2 9BA
Tel: 01423 501 041
Web: www.htcuk.org click on Easter revision
Email study@htcuk.org
Medical sciences preparation

Imperial College, University of London

Exhibition Road, London, SW7 2AZ
Tel 020 7594 8043
Web: www.ic.ac.uk
Email: schliaison@ic.ac.uk
10 day Masterclass in Medical and Biological Sciences, for
Year 12 students, Summer. Part of the Exscitec programme.
For those interested in a career in Medicine.
See www.excitec.com/masterclass2005

Irwin College

164 London Road, Leicester LE2 IND
Tel: 0116 255 2648
Web: www.cife.org.uk/irwin/index.htm
Email: enquiries@irwincollege.tele2.co.uk
Foundation course in medical science prepares students for an entrance exam set by the universities in the Czech Republic. Successful students transfer to a six year degree in Medicine or Dentistry.

Landsdowne Independent 6th Form College

40-44 Bark Place, London W2 4AT
Tel: 020 7616 4400
Web: www.lansdownecollege.com
Email: education@lansdownecollege.com
Medical sciences preparation

Mander Portman Woodward

90-92 Queen's Gate, London SW7 5AB
Tel: 0207 835 1355
Web: www.mpw.co.uk (plus links to other MPW centres)
Email: london@mpw.co.uk
Medical sciences preparation

Revision courses outside the UK

Art History

Art History Abroad

179c New Kings Road, London SW6 4SW
Tel: 020 7731 2231

Web: www.arthistoryabroad.com
Email: Info@arthistoryabroad.com
Locations: Florence, Rome, Paris and London
Easter revision courses in History of art AS and A2. Also
Summer holiday course to supplement A level study.

Languages

British Institute of Florence

Palazzo Strozzino, Piazza Strozzi, 2, I-50123 Florence, Italy
Tel: (00 39) 055 2677 8200
Web: www.britishinstitute.it
Email: info@britishinstitute.it
AS and A2 Italian : 5 day overviewcourses held at Easter.

Cactus Language

4 Clarence House, 30-31 North Street, Brighton BN1 1EB
Tel: 01273 725 200
Web: www.cactuslanguage.com
Email: enquiry@cactuslanguage.com
French intensive A level revision course held in Winter (Biarrritz)
and Summer (Bordeaux). Private tuition also possible.

Caledonia Languages Abroad

Bonnington Mill, 72 Newhaven Road, Edinburgh EH6 5QG
Tel: 0131 621 7721/2
Web: www.caledonialanguages.co.uk
Email: courses@caledonialanguages.co.uk
A level French revision courses in Nice

Cesa Languages Abroad

CESA House, Pennance Road, Lanner, Cornwall TR16 5TQ
Tel: 01209 2118
Web: www.cesalanguages.com
Email: info@cesalanguages.com
Easter courses in Nice and Madrid. Summer courses in Madrid, Nice and Biarritz. Spanish and French. Private tuition can be arranged for German, Spanish, French, Italian and others for AS and A2 exams (various locations.)

Challenge UK

101 Lorna Road, Hove, Sussex, BN3 3EL
Tel: 01273 208648
Web: www.challengeuk.com
Email: via website
AS/A2 French revision, half-terms, Easter and Summer. Various locations in France.

En Famille Overseas

4 St Helena Road, Colchester CO3 3BA
Tel: 01206 546 741
Web: www.enfamilleoverseas.sageweb.co.uk
Email: enfamilleoverseas@btopenworld.com
Loire Coaching centre, France. Two week A level revision course in summer holidays. 4 students stay 'en famille' with tutor and family.

Languages Abroad

67 Ashby Road, Loughborough, Leicestershire LE11 3AA
Tel: 01509 211612
Web: www.languagesabroad.co.uk
Email: info@languagesabroad.co.uk

Language schools in many locations including Latin America. A level revision in nine languages.

Living Spanish

10 Barley Mow Passage, Chiswick, London W4 4PH
Tel: 020 8747 2018
Web: www.livingspanish.com

Privtate Tutors

This small selection of sites is an introduction to the locating of private tutors. Many of theses tutors will provide email/web-based tuition and coaching, as well as the conventional home visit or college-based services. Inclusion in these listings does not imply any form of recommendation; parents and students are urged to research into issues such as academic/teaching qualifications of tutors and 'police-checking' before employing any form of private tutor. Some sites state that all their tutors have had all such matters checked before their inclusion on the site listing.

A + tutors

A web directory of UK private tutors and online tutors
Web: www.aplustutors.co.uk
Clickable map of UK to help location

Gabbitas Educational Consultants

Web: www.gabbitas.co.uk
Fill in an online form to find 'Gabbitas-listed private tutors within the London area'

Personal Tutors

Cheadle House, Cheadle, Cheshire SK8 1AH
Tel: 0161 428 2285
Web: www.personal-tutors.co.uk
Free lists of local tutors to help with exam preparation/revision

Tutors International

Suite 2, 28 Walton Lane, Oxford, OX1 2JN
Tel: 01865 435
Web: www.goalover.com/tutors
Tutors to help students prepare for exams.

Wise Owl Tuition

176a Mitcham Lane, London SW16 6NS
Tel: 020 8769 4546
Web: www.wiseowltuition.co.uk
Private tuition in all subjects from GCSE- A level- degree study.
Must be 18+ to make bookings.

Online tuition and interactive revision websites

Please see Section 3

Revision websites

In the past few years there has been, and continues to be, a huge output of web-based resources on revision theory and technique, individual subject information, course materials and interactive tutorial sites. Many of these sites offer initial information without charge, although a number of websites require registration, and charge for more detailed services.

Websites included in these listings are simply a selection of those available: inclusion does not imply recommendation nor does exclusion imply the opposite. There are simply too many sites for all to be listed and evaluation is not possible in this publication.

There is no totally foolproof way to ensure the safety, quality or credibility or websites. However, many of them are run by 'household names' such as the BBC, Channel 4, national newspapers, educational bodies etc. If you want to reassure yourself about the site credentials you could check the following:

- **Site ownership** It may be possible to find out who owns, manages and monitors a site - this information may be available from an 'about us' link

- **How up-to-date** Individual sections may indicate a revision date, although a single 'last updated' date on the home page of a website is rarely a guide to how up-to-date the detailed content is.

- **Popularity** The number of site 'hits' may give an approximate indication of popularity, although a 'site counter' is unlikely to distinguish between regular site users and automated hits.

- **Accreditation** Accreditation logos or messages may be displayed on the home page - if so, who is the accrediting body?

- **Payment precautions** If payment is requested for any services, you may wish to check on the 'security of payment over the Internet' details which should be described on the site. Check also if your browser window is displaying a 'secure server' symbol at the payment request stage. Your internet service provider should be able to advise you about these security issues. If you are cautious about site authenticity in any way, you may prefer to use just the free part of the site.

- **Chat rooms and online discussions** Be cautious.

- **Advice** Look at a websites such as www.webSafeCrackerz.com which is a site for teenagers designed by teenagers and gives some advice on safe use of the Internet. www.childline.org.uk also has a section on safe surfing.

National Grid for Learning

The NGfL is the 'gateway to educational resources on the Internet'. Launched in November 1998 as part of the government strategy to help learners and teachers in the UK benefit from ICT (Information and communications technology). The NGFL site is funded by the Department for Education and Skills (DfES) and managed by BECTA.

For officially recommended revision websites go to www.ngfl.gov.uk then go to Search then Revision. Here you will find the NGFL guide list of recommended revision sites.

Readers who are parents of a minor may wish to read the following section.

Parental advice on safe use of the internet by minors

The Internet is an unregulated medium and parents will want to ensure the safe use of this medium by their children. Some sites dealing with this issue are:

- **www.childnet-int.org** which is one of a number of charities working on the issue of Internet safety and the 13-16 year old user.

- **www.WebSafeCrackerz.com** which is described as the 'first child safety site designed by teens for teens'. The site deals with every aspect of risk associated with surfing the Net.

- **www.kidsmart.org.uk** deals with all aspects of Internet safety

- **www.parentalk.co.uk** click on Internet safety

- **www.parentsonline.gov.uk** Free Home Office booklet available 'Keep your child safe on the Internet' - order from 0870 2414680 or read online.

Despite the 'alert' messages above and the need to advise minors to be cautious when using the Internet, it is nevertheless a marvellous and instantaneous resource offering invaluable revision support

Listed websites are divided into three sub-sections:

Overvie sites providing introductions to the topic across a wide range of subjects, plus links to other revision sites

Subject-specific sites providing information and course materials: many of these will also be interactive sites - see below

Interactive sites providing services such as on-screen self-assessment or tutor assessment with feedback. Any fees payable should be clearly indicated on the site home page.

Overview sites covering all examination subjects

- **www.activerevision.com**

Click on Revision – offers free tips and hints.

- **www.bbc.co.uk**

Go to schools/gcse/bitesize. Online revision help in a wide range of GCSE subjects and tests with immediate feedback. Also on same website follow links to AS and A level revision skills and to Onion Street for a comprehensive overview of the topic of Study skills.

- **www.bbc.co.uk/radio1/onelife**

Select Education then Revision.
General advice pages, revision tips and planners.

- **www.broadoak.n-somerset.sch.uk**

Wide ranging revision advice, exam tips, revision notes from Broadoak Community school.

- **www.channel4.com**

Go to Homework/Revision. Links to their recommended revision and coursework sites for GCSE/A level/Scottish Highers/I.B.

- **www.coursework.info**

34 subjects at GCSE, As, A2 and I.B. levels: documents, essays and coursework examples. Chargeable site or free access if you provide three pieces of your own coursework to the site.

Websites

• www.dulwich.org.uk/gateway/revision.html

Overview site which evaluates other revision sites • **www. eastercourses.info**

Database of Easter revision courses for GCSE and A level.

• www.hotcourses.com

Revision notes for 11 GCSE subjects - follow revision link.

• www.kevinsplayroom.co.uk

Click on subject required or go straight to Study support section.

• www.learn.co.uk

Revision guide for wide range of GCSE subjects. Online lessons and tests. Special section for boys, with parental tips and hints. Site owned by Guardian newspaper.

• www.lettsed.co.uk

Study and revision support.

• www.ngfl.org.uk

National Grid for Learning 'overview' site on Revision with links to recommended websites.

• www.projectgcse.co.uk

Revision/coursework resources and links for main GCSE subjects.

• www.projectalevel.co.uk

Revision resources and links for seven main A level subjects.

• www.projecteducation.co.uk

Detailed links directory.

• www.revisiontime.com

Websites and resources for wide range of GCSE and A level subjects.

• www.revisionlink.co.uk

Click on your choice of 13 subjects to find links to subject-specific sites.

• www.revisioncentral.co.uk

Overview site: links to revision sites by subject and exam levels.

- ## www.revision-notes.co.uk

Revision note for a GCSE,A level and IB. Wide range of subjects.

- ## www.revise.it

Online revision guide covering 6 subjects.

- ## www.samlearning.com

Free revision materials for limited period of time then subscription service for GCSE/ A level help and advice.

- ## www.s-cool.co.uk

Revision and course materials and handy hints on exam techniques

- ## www.schoolshistory.org.uk

Go to Revise, here you'll find links to 6 core school subjects with revision tests and hints and coursework advice.

- ## www.schoolzone.co.uk

Free worksheets and resources on wide range of subjects

- ## www.study-links.com

As it sounds, links to subject and revision sites

- ## www.ukexams.com

For special exam courses, past exam papers, private tutors- links and revision information go to Ukexams email: contact@ukexams.com

Subject-specific information sites

A selection from a wide variety of available sites

Biology, Chemistry and Physics

- ## www.examstutor.co.uk

Go to Revision section. A level revision guides, chargeable site - annual subscription per subject.

- ## www.mrothery.co.uk

AS and A2 AQA board Biology: resources, past papers. Mock exams marked and scored for small fee. www.mrothery.co.uk

Business Studies

- **www.osl-ltd.co.uk/tutor**

Free online tuition for A level Business studies

- **www.examsututor.co.uk**

Chargeable revision guide to Business studies A level

Computing/Information Technology

- **www.computingstudents.com**

AS /A2 level computing revision materials. Chat room.

- **www.ictgcse.com**

Information technology resources

Design Technology

www.design-technology.org

Free handouts, online lessons and much more

Economics

- **www.tutor2u.com**

Free revision briefings online For GCSE and , AS and A2 Economics. Discussion boards.

- **www.osl-ltd.co.uk**

Economics revision notes

English

- **www.englishbiz.co.uk**

Comprehensive revision site for English GCSE and A level

- **www.eriding.net**

Go to Revising Language issues and stylistics. Help for those revising AS and A2 English Language

French

- **www.frenchrevision.co.uk**

Aimed at 11-18s, self-scorable oral and written exercises

Websites

- **www.languagesonline.org.uk**

Interactive exercises and immediate feedback on tests/exercises

Geography
- **www.geoexplorer.co.uk**

Go to revision section

German
- **www.atschool.eduweb.co.uk**

Interactive exercises, notes, exercises, oral exercise, video material
- **www.languagesonline.org.uk**

Interactive exercises and immediate feedback on tests/exercises

History
- **www.learnhistory.org.uk**

Lessons, revision content, quizzes and research help
- **www.educationforum.co.uk**

GCSE History- links to all exam boards and options. Downloadable revision guides, tests and activities
- **www.thehistorysite.co.uk**

GCSE History revision downloadable guides

Italian
- **www.languagesonline.org.uk**

Interactive exercises and immediate feedback on tests/exercises

Law
- **www.law-tuition.co.uk**

Law GCSE and AS/A2 courses lists, model answers, revision cassettes

Maths
- **www.examstutor.co.uk**

A level revision guide. Chargeable site by annual subscription

- ### *www.iscis.uk.net*
Numberworks specializes in Maths tuition for Years 1-11, revision help from SATs through to GCSEs.

- ### *www.mathsrevision.net*
Comprehensive, free revision notes for GCSE and A level maths students

- ### *www.gcsemaths.fsnet.co.uk*
GCSE Maths. Lessons, games, tests, worksheets

- ### *www.mathsa.fsnet.co.uk*
Similar to above, but for A level Maths.

Media studies
www.barrycomp.com
GCSE, AS and A2 revision materials

Music
- ### *www.musicatschool.co.uk*
A level resources/ Edexcel syllabus

- ### *www.abcmusicnotes.com*
GCSE, AS and A2 course work, essay help, exam hints, revision help

- ### *www.gwhite.co.uk/music*
Masses of revision info on this music site

Physical Education
- ### *www.physicaleducation.co.uk*
Resources for GSCE and A level

Psychology
Several of the overview sites listed above cover Psychology

Physics
www.cyberphysics.pwp.blueyonder.co.uk
Physics revision notes

Websites

Religious Studies

- *http://members.fortunecity.com/rsrevision*
Revision notes for AS Religious studies, OCR exam board

- *www.paulhopkins.org.uk*
GCSE Religious studies, packed with revision information

Sociology

- *www.barrycomp.com*
GCSE, AS and A2 revision materials; also downloadable detailed revision guide

Spanish

- *www.studyspanish.com*
Four sections: pronunciation, Grammar, vocabulary, verb drills and online translator. Also quizzes, tests, exam exercises, oral exercises.

- *www.languagesonline.org.uk*
Interactive exercises and immediate feedback on tests/exercises

Interactive and tutorial sites

A small selection of the enormous and proliferating number of such sites; many of the sites listed above also offer interactive facilities.

All subjects

- *www.ASW2.net*
36-38 Kensington Park Road London W11 3BU
Tel: 020 8339 1256

Described as the UK's only online A level school. Revision practice, exam tips and techniques ,exam practice, essay writing. For AS and A2 levels. Fee level (2004) approx £350 for 10 hours online tuition. Personal online tuition available throughout school year. School is operated and owned by Southbank International, an independent school. Teaching materials were prepared by teachers.

An A level course consists of 200 online lessons. UK-based students can do Science lab work at the Southbank school in London.

Websites

• www.revision-notes.co.uk

Interactive site- members of the public, teachers and former students all encouraged to post their notes for everyone to read

• www.studysuccess.co.uk

Interactive site. Home of ExamGenie, mnemonics-based revision tool

• www.uk-tutors.com

Described as the UK's 'first model answer' tuition service for A level students. Answers supplied to A level essay queries, coursework and exam questions. Site carries warning about plagiarism.

Biology

• www.mrothery.co.uk

AS and A2 AQA Board mock exams assessed and scored for a moderate fee

British Home Tutors

• www.bht.co.uk

Email: enquiries@bht.co.uk. Private tuition at students or tutors home, or by email if preferred

Chat-rooms

• www.gcseforums.com
• www.alevelforums.com

History

• www.schoolshistory.org.uk/revision.htm

GCSE history links to interactive revision exercises and lessons. Also articles on Study skills with links.

Law

• www.law-tuition.co.uk

'Personalised revision and distance-learning facilities for Law GCSE and A level courses.

Maths

- **www.mathsmasters.com**

Sudents look here for comprehensive revision services ranging from crash courses/online tutoring, email helpline and revision lesson bank.

- **www.examtutors.co.uk**

Online access to teachers and lecturers in science and Maths subjects, by annual subscription. Information sections free.

Languages

- **www.languagesonline.org.uk**

Interactive exercises and immediate feedback on tests/exercises.

- **www.studyspanish.com**

Interactive exercises

- **www.frenchexams.co.uk**

AS level French, past papers which can be used with all Boards.

Sciences

- **www.examtutors.co.uk**

Online access to teachers and lecturers in science and Maths subjects, by annual subscription - free nformation sections.

A selection of the many subject revision guides, textbooks, CD-ROM and multimedia products on revision theories and techniques

Selected books about revision theories and techniques

- **Rev up for Revision** by Tony Buzan
Publisheed HarperCollins; ISBN 000717702X

- **How to Improve Your Memory** by Robert Leach
Published National Extension College; ISBN 1853564796

- **How to Manage Your Study Time** by Roger lewis
Published National Extension College; ISBN: 0003223647

- **How to Study Effectively** by Richard Freeman
Published National Extension College; ISBN: 1853568163

- **How to Write Essays** by Roger Lewis
Published National Extension College; ISBN: 1853568155

- **Learning CHAMPS** by Colin Rose, Anne Civardi
Sterling Publishing; ISBN: 0806990325

- **The Student's Guide to Exam Success** by Eileen Tracy
Published Open University Press; ISBN 0 335 20726 X

- **Write Great Essays** by Peter Levin
Published Open University Press; ISBN 0 335 21577 7

- **Successful Teamwork** by Peter Levin
Published Open University Press; ISBN 0 335 21578 5

- **Sail Through Exams** by Peter Levin
Published Open University Press; ISBN 0 335 21576 9

- **Memletics Accelerated Learning Manual** by Sean Whitely
Details at www.memletics.com/manual

- **Accelerated Learning for the 21st Century** by Colin Rose
Published DTP; ISBN: 0440507790

- **Accelerated Learning Handbook** by Dave Meier
  Published Berrett-Koehler; ISBN 0071355472
- **Accelerated Learning in Practice** by Alastair Smith
  Published Network Educational Press Ltd; ISBN 1855390485
- **Effective Learning Activities** by Chris Dickinson
  Published Network Educational Press Ltd; ISBN 1855390353
- **Essential Study Skills** by Sandra Simfield
  Published Sage Publications; ISBN 0761949585

Revision subject guides

There are several ' revision-by- subject' series by various publishers. examples include:

- **Letts exam and revision guides**
- **Oxford revision guides**
- **GCSE Bitesize (BBC) guides**
- **Dorling Kindersley guides**
- **Co-ordination group publications**
- **Collins guides**

All good bookshops will sell these, or they can be located/ordered online on websites such as Amazon, Trotman, BBC shop and Times online.

- **Homeschooling books**

This series of titles links academic subjects to individual learning styles. See www.homeschoolingbooks.com for further details: this site also incluides a learning style 'assessment tool'.

Revision packs

- **Exam Genie Revision system**

This is designed for GCSE/AS/A2 revision. See www.tutor2u for details: select online store to order.

Multimedia presentations

- **Improve SAT and GCSE results (CHAMPS)**

CD-ROM described as a product that will 'teach 10-16 yr olds a range of effective learning techniques including: revision strategies, successful exam-taking'. See www.acceleratedlearning.com for further information:select CHAMPS.

- **Master it Faster**

CD-ROM based on techniques described in the book of the same title by Colin Rose. Includes Learning Maps, memory techniques etc.

- **CD-roms on various exam subjects**

These are produced by well-known publishers such as the BBC, OUP, Dorling-Kindersley etc.

Video

- **AS Guru Study skills**

AS guru English, Biology and other similar titles, available from BBCshop www.bbcshop.com

Courses

Run by the Buzan centre, Champs and others. For further information see websites such as:

- **www.mind-map.com** go to mind map for kids courses
- **www.mind-mapping.co.uk**
- **www.illumine.co.uk**
- **www.acceleratedlearning.com**

Revision techniques and theories

We are unique individuals and each of us has our own way of learning, memorising, revising and then, recalling knowledge in order to answer examination questions. This section provides a brief overview of some of the major learning or revision theories and techniques and refers to a selection of information resources, mainly web-based. Relevant books are to be found in the previous section.

How do our brains work whilst studying and learning ?

What goes on inside our brains whilst we are learning and memorising information? There are thousands of surveys and reports by experts on this topic which concur that:

- *The upper part of our brains is divided into two halves, left and right side. For most of us the left half deals with logic, words, lists, numbers, linearity, analysis etc. The right half deals with rhythm, imagination, colour, day-dreaming, spatial awareness and dimension. Many studies have shown that the more we use both sides of our brain, the more effective our overall brain performance becomes.*

- *Experts on learning and the brain concur that 'active learning' involves constructing our own meanings to what we are taught or read or hear. Linking to what we already know, we invent our own concepts and ideas - a theory of learning called Constructivism or 'meaning-making'. Learners make mistakes and omissions when constructing their learning- revising your learning can uncover these.*

- *Therefore, learning combines what you already know with what you want to know and links this new information within your store of knowledge. Your memory will then process these new links and associations to be recalled later when you need them.*

- *Every time you learn something, your brain changes physically. The brain is like a muscle, the more it is exercised, the stronger it gets.*

For further information, go to:

- *http://encarta.msn.com Click on encyclopaedia articles. Search on brain then Memory (psychology) and Learning.*

- **www.sciencemuseum.org.uk/exhibitions/brain**
- **www.enlightenedlearning.co.uk** Go to articles then The Brain, select topics.
- **www.brainybusiness.com** Go to articles, then to Developing your mind
- **www.acceleratedlearning.com** Go to What is accelerated learning and follow links.

Learning Styles

Do you know which senses you prefer to use as you learn? Do you know your preferred/dominant 'learning style'? .

There is some controversy over the notion of a 'learning style for life'. Some theorists state that Learning Styles are not fixed and that we can all develop our lesser-used styles; others state that our dominant Learning Style is fixed from birth. These theorists believe that this 'fixed' style will guide the way we learn, change the way we internally memorise/visualise our experiences, the way we recall information and even influence the words we choose to use. Other theorists state that we adopt different Learning Styles in different circumstances.

(i) A recent report identified 71 models of Learning styles and evaluated 13 of the most influential. [†] The report is a critical evaluation of the different models and urges caution when labelling learners as one 'type' or another. The researchers note that Learning style questionnaires are widely used in Further and Higher education but that some of the best known have low reliability, poor validity and ought to be discontinued. They conclude that the use of reliable and valid models is of overriding importance.

See www.lsda.org.uk go to Publications, search on Learning styles. This will take you to 'Learning styles and pedagogy in post-16 learning', ([†] p.139 Table 44) February 2004. The entire report is downloadable, free.

(ii) However, there does appear to be widespread consensus amongst the various theorists/models that learning style preferences do exist. For example:

- *Solitary/ reflective (preference for working alone/likes self-study)*
- *Interpersonal/social (preference for learning in groups/with others)*
- *Physical/kinaesthetic (preference for using body, hands and touch)*
- *Linguistic/verbal (preference for using words, both in speech and in writing)*
- *Mathematical/logical (preference for using logic, reasoning and systems)*
- *Visual/spatial (preference for using pictures, images and spatial understanding)*
- *Musical/aural (preference for using sound and music)*

(iii) Bearing in mind the need to exercise caution over the results, readers may like to take an online questionnaire/test and discover their Learning Style(s). The following are some of the sites where you complete a Learning styles questionnaire and get immediate response results:

- **www.learning-styles-online.com**
- **www.acceleratedlearning.com**   *Go to What is my personal learning style?*
- **www.engr.ncsu.edu/learningstyles**   *Go to Index of Learning styles questionnaire.44 questions, instant feedback report.*
- **www.learntolearn.org**
- **www.creative.learningcentre.com**   *Go to Learning style questionnaire*

(iv) Additionally, many theorists agree that the way individuals prefer to learn determines how they want to receive new information:

- *Some want the overview first; others want the details straight away*
- *Some like information presented in text/speech; others want pictures*
- *Some learn better by doing; others want to reflect before acting*
- *Some need to understand the theory; others prefer to 'get on with it'.*

Techniques

(v) According to some educationalists, for maximum effectiveness, revision style(s) should match preferred learning style(s). For example,

- ***www.acceleratedlearning.com** features a course called CHAMPS that states its objective as being to 'help students match their learning style to learning techniques', including revision style and exam technique. This is also featured on*
- ***www.learntolearn.org/index_uk.htm***

vi). According to some theorists, each preferred learning style uses a different part of the brain. Researchers using brain-imaging technology have discovered the key areas of the brain that is responsible for each learning style.

Learning style	Area of brain used
Solitary/reflective	Frontal and parietal lobes and limbic system
Interpersonal/social	Frontal and temporal lobes, limbic system
Physical/kinaesthetic	Cerebellum and motor cortex
Verbal/linguistic	Temporal and frontal lobes
Mathematical/Logical	Parietal lobes
Social	Frontal/temporal lobes and limbic system
Visual/spatial	Occipital lobes at back of brain manage visual senses; parietal and occipital lobes manage spatial senses
Musical/aural	Temporal lobes, especially the right lobe

*Go to **www.learning-styles-online.com** for further details.*

(vii) For further research studies/reports on the concept of Learning Styles, look at:

- ***http://ferl.becta.org.uk/display.cfm?resid=7543** Introduction to Learning styles*
- ***www.lsda.org.uk** - insert 'learning style' into the search box*

- **www.standards.dfes.gov.uk** - *insert 'learning style' into the search box*
- **www.helpisathand.gov.uk** - *insert 'learning style' into the search box*
- **www.ngfl.gov.uk** - *insert 'learning style' into the search box*

Study skills and techniques

There are a whole range of recognised 'study skills', including revision skills. Some sites to look at include:

- **www.lettsed.co.uk** click on Revision-Study
- **www.activerevision.com**
- **www.enlightenedlearning.co.uk**
- **www.bbc.co.uk/schools** Go to Revision then to Onion Street
- **www.learning-study-skills.com**
- **www.studygs.net**
- **www.samlearning.com** Go to GCSEs/A levels. Follow on-screen prompts.

Many of the websites listed in Section 3 of this book will also include information on study and revision skills and many include online 'self-assessment/self-discovery' tests.

Mind maps, concept maps and graphic organisers

There appears to be considerable overlap between the above revision methods; many of the websites mentioned below cover all three, using an integrated approach.

Mind Maps

Scientific research which began in the 1950s into the workings of the human brain developed into the concept/technique of the Mind map, developed in the 1960s by Tony Buzan. He in turn had been inspired by Thomas Edison's theories of creativity and brain organisation. Essentially, Tony Buzan claims that Mind Mapping aims to tackle a basic educational problem: that we are taught what to think before we are taught HOW to think. The Mind map is a powerful graphic technique which can be used in every part

of life where improved learning and clearer thinking will improve/ maximise human performance. It uses the entire range of the brain's cortical skills such as: word, image, number, logic, rhythm, colour and spatial awareness. Mind Maps are now used globally by millions of people of all ages, in education, training and industry. Mind Maps can be drawn either by hand or using software; the former method is a personal tool and utilises the kinaesthetic senses and helps the learner memorise and retrieve information later on. The latter method is more useful when communicating ideas to other people. see www.schoolmaps.demon.co.uk for details. Other websites to look at include:

- **http://mindtools.com** Go to Mind maps and Memory Improvements

- **www.mind-map.com** Go to Buzan courses and resources for explanations of how to create and use a mind-map, including use of images. The site also lists details of 2-day Mind-mapping courses.

- **www.mindgenius.com** Go to Education

- **www.examstutor.co.uk** Go to revision techniques then to Mind-mapping

Concept maps and Graphical organisers

These have their origin in the learning movement called Constructivism. Constructivists believe that prior knowledge is used as a framework to use new knowledge and that the way we think influences how and what we learn. Concept maps identify the way we think, the way we see relationships between knowledge. Using a concept map involves thinking in terms of key words or symbols that will represent ideas and words. They include:

- **Tree/hierarchy diagrams** (information is presented in a descending order of importance with the most important placed at the top of the 'tree')

- **Organisational charts**

- **Spider diagrams/spidergrams** (Spidergrams, for example, have a heading as the main topic/theme in the centre of the map with lines/legs coming out from the 'body' representing linked ideas or topics)

- other forms of graphical organisation methods such as: webbing, matrix, flow-charts, clustering/cycle, interaction outline, storyboard, compare/contrast, family tree, Venn diagrams, KWLH technique.

Specialist forms of concept maps include: picture landscapes/3-D and mandala maps.

Some websites to look at:

- **www.schoolmaps.demon.co.uk** Go to Mapping techniques
- **www.inspiration.com** Go to visual learning techniques
- **www.smartdraw.com** Go to Tutorials, education:mind and concept maps
- **www.studygs.net/mapping** Go to concept or mind-mapping
- **www.bradford.ac.uk** Sach by exams and revision tips
- **www.examstutor.co.uk** Go to Revision: revision techniques: The Index study system

Mnemonics

A mnemonic is a way of helping you remember information using abbreviations, words and phrases. For example, to remember the seven colours of the rainbow, you might make up a sentence/ abbreviation containing the letters R (red), O (orange), Y (yellow),G (green) , B (blue), I (indigo), V (violet) ie. Richard of York gave battle in vain. You would then learn this sentence off by heart and use it to recall the seven colours when you needed to.

Memletics

This is an integrated learning system containing over 80 techniques concerned with accelerated learning. A 'technique selection matrix' helps you match the material you are learning to techniques that can help.

- **www.memletics.com** Also publish the Memletics manual

Exercising your brain cells (Neurobics)

All day, every day, our brains are activated by your senses and we are constantly bombarded by new stimuli. Try exercising your brain by learning/doing something new ie. If you always write with your right hand, try writing with your left for a while. Changing the hand you write with will exercise the large network of connections, circuits and brain areas not normally used on the opposite side of the brain! Brain exercises are known as neurobics (as distinct from aerobics!).

Further information:

- ***www.neurobics.com*** *Go to 'Keep your brain alive / Brain exercises*
- ***www.themindgym.com***

Accreditation of course providers: guide to organisations/ acronyms

BAC

British Accreditation Council for Further and Higher Education

BAC is a registered charity established in 1984 to act as the impartial, national, accrediting body for independent further and higher education. BAC now accredits colleges across the globe, as well as 160+ colleges in the UK. Institutions are fully inspected every five years and receive an interim inspection after 2-3 years. Details of accredited institutions can be viewed on the website. www.thecapability.uk.com/bac

CIFE

Council for Independent Further Education
Web: www.cife.org.uk or www.getthegrade.co.uk

CIFE is a professional association representing 27 accredited independent 6th form and tutorial colleges. These are usually aimed at the 16+ student. Between them, the CIFE colleges offer teaching in 86 different subjects areas.

Full membership of CIFE is only open to colleges which are accredited by BAC or ISC (see below). Regular inspections are carried out by BAC, the ISC, and where appropriate, the DfES (Department for Education and Skills.)

The CIFE guide is downloadable, free or charge, from the website.

ISC

Independent School Council
Web: www.iscis.uk.net

ISC provides an official website for the 1,300 UK schools accredited by the *Independent Schools Council*. The *Independent Schools Inspectorate* was established in April 2000 and is recognised both by the DfES and monitored by Ofsted (see below).

Under Section 163 of the Education Act 2000, a school must pass the *Independent Schools Inspectorate (ISI)* accreditation inspection to qualify for membership of the ISC. Independent schools not in membership of the ISC are inspected by Ofsted and are known as 'non-association' schools.

Schools are re-inspected every six years. ISI Inspection reports are published and available on www.isiinspect.org.uk: go to School inspection reports.

ODLQC

Open and Distance Learning Quality Council
Web: www.odlqc.org.uk

Accrediting body for open and distance education, providing ccreditation of providers of home study, distance-learning, online or e-learning or other open or flexible learning courses. A downloadable copy of the ODLQC's 'Buyers guide to distance learning' is available from the website. The site also lists all accredited providers.

Ofsted

Office for Standards in Education
Web: www.ofsted.gov.uk

Ofsted is responsible for inspecting all schools and all 14-19 education in England. Independent schools not in ISC membership are also subject to Ofsted inspection. To locate inspection reports go to www.ofsted.gov.uk and click on Colleges and post-16. Reports are subdivided into: Further education colleges, Independent schools or Independent special schools.

Accreditation

Schools and college inspection reports

Inspection reports and associated information about schools and colleges in Scotland, Wales, Northern Ireland is available as follows:

- ***Scotland*** *www.hmie.gov.uk*
- ***Wales*** *www.estyn.gov.uk*
- ***Northern Ireland*** *www.deni.gov.uk/inspection_services*

Examination Boards

QCA

Qualifications and Curriculum Authority
Web: qca.org.uk

QCA maintains and develops the national curriculum and associated assessments, tests and exams; accredits and monitors qualifications in colleges and at work.

Contact details: Customer relations, 83 Piccadilly, London W1 8QA Tel 020 7509 5555 or email info@qca.org.uk

For the QCA in Northern Ireland email: infoni@qca.org.uk

The QCA have established a website for 14-19 yr olds and learning: go to www.qca.org.uk/14-19/

Awarding bodies

There are various awarding bodies offering general qualifications

ENGLAND
- **AQA, Edexcel** and **OCR** (These three bodies are regulated by the QCA - see above)

WALES
- **WJEC** (regulated by the QCA for Wales)

NORTHERN IRELAND
- **CCEA** (self-regulatory body)

SCOTLAND
- **SQA**

Contact details for individual examination boards

- **AQA**

Assessment and Qualifications Alliance. This Board was formed in 1997 from an alliance of the AEB, SEG, City and Guilds and NEAB.

Address: Staghill House, Guildford, Surrey GU2 7 XJ
Tel: 01483 506506   Email: mailbox@aqa.org.uk
Web: www.aqa.org.uk
A link from the site takes you to past exam question papers and
mark schemes. email mailbox@aqa.org.uk Printed copies are also
available by post from the Publications department.

- ### EDEXCEL

Formed in 1996 by a merger of BTEC and ULEAC.
Address: Stewart House, 32 Russell Square, London WC1B 5DN
Tel: 0870 240 9800   Email: enquiries@edexcel.org.uk
Web: www.edexcel.org.uk

- ### OCR

Oxford, Cambridge and RSA exams

Formed in 1998 from UCLES and the RSA. For queries relating to
general qualifications, tel 01223 553998 or email helpdesk@ocr.
org.uk. For enquiries relating to vocational qualifications, tel: 024 76
851509 or email cib@ocr.org.uk

- ### CCEA

Council for Curriculum Exams and Assessment
Address: 29 Clarendon Dock, Clarendon Road, Belfast, BT1 3BG
Tel 028 9026 1200 or email info@ccea.org.uk
Web: www.ccea.org.uk - has links to exams and accreditation.

- ### WJEC

Welsh Joint Education Committee
Examining board offering A level/AS, GCSE and CEA exams.
Address 245, Western Avenue, Cardiff CF5 2YX
Tel: 029 2026 5000   Email: exams@wjec.co.uk
Web: www.wjec.co.uk

- ### SQA

Scottish Qualifications Authority.
The national body in Scotland responsible for the development,
accreditation, assessment and certification of qualifications other
than degrees.www.sqa.org.uk
Address Scottish QCA, 25 Douglas street, Glasgow G2 7NQ
Tel: 0845 279 1000   Email: customer@sqa.org.uk
Web: www.sqa.org.uk

- **IBO**

International Baccalaureate Organisation

Founded in 1968, the IBO works with 1,426 schools across 117 countries offering the three-level IB programme.
Web: www.ibo.org   Email: ibhq@ibo.org or www.ibsca.org.uk
IB schools and colleges in the UK and Ireland.

- **JCQ**

Joint Council for Qualifications

Represents the major awarding bodies which serve England, Wales, Northern Ireland and Scotland. Includes the AQA, CCEA, City and Guilds, Edexcel, OCR, SQA and the WJEC above. It came into operation in January 2004.
Veritas House, Finsbury pavement, London EC2A 1NQ
Tel: 020 7 638 4125   Email info@jcq.org.uk

Awarding bodies A- Z

An alphabetical list of awarding bodies can be found at www.dfes.gov.uk: click on Section 96 for ' approved general qualifications for those aged 19 and under, Awarding bodies', Section 97 for 'approved vocational qualifications for people aged 19+, awarding bodies'

Past examination papers

Essential for revision purposes! Your school/college should be able to provide you with copies of recent past exam papers. If you have left education, or are studying independently, you could contact the relevant examination board or check out their websites, above. Several have links to downloadable past exam papers.

Phobic about exams?

The national phobias website carries lots of helpful information about tackling stress and anxiety and provides a free email confidential support and enquiry service. Go to www.phobics-society. org.uk or email natphob.soc@good.co.uk.

Don't forget to talk to your teachers/lecturers, student counsellor/mentor/personal tutor - all of whom will be able to help and advise you.

INDEX

Index